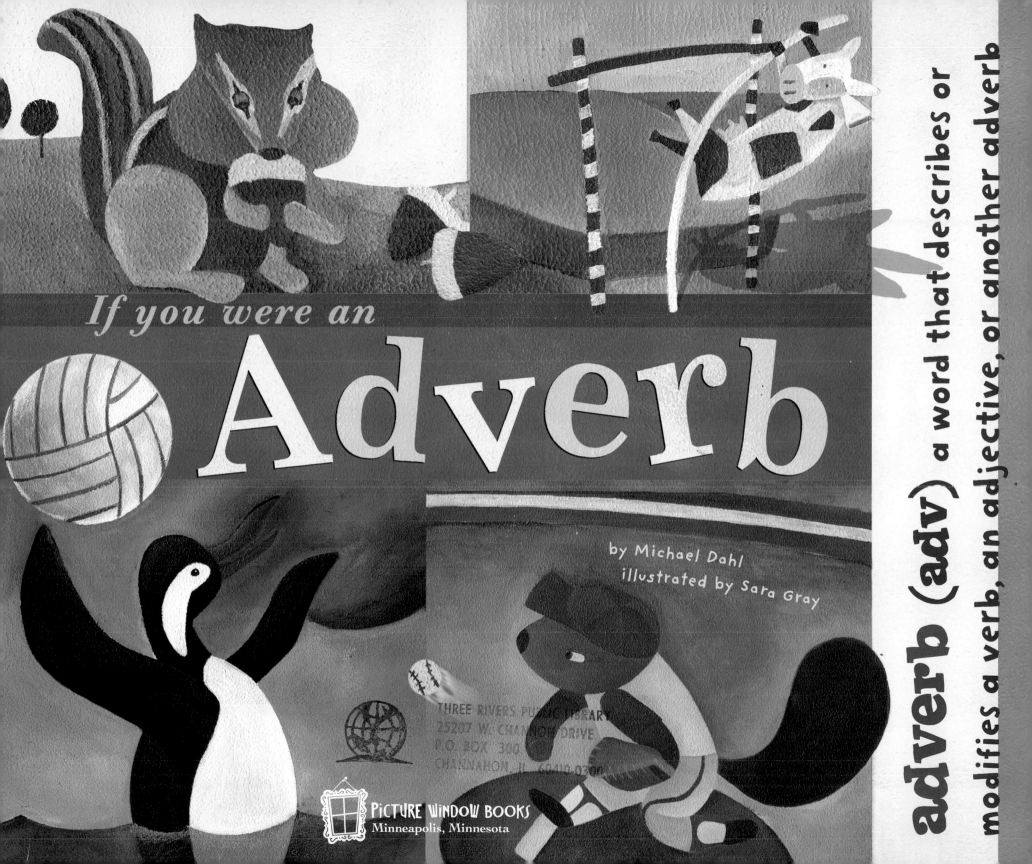

If you were an Adverb

by Michael Dahl
illustrated by Sara Gray

PICTURE WINDOW BOOKS
Minneapolis, Minnesota

adverb (adv) a word that describes or modifies a verb, an adjective, or another adverb

Editor: Christianne Jones
Designer: Nathan Gassman
Page Production: Tracy Kaehler
Creative Director: Keith Griffin
Editorial Director: Carol Jones
The illustrations in this book
were created with acrylics.

Picture Window Books
5115 Excelsior Boulevard
Suite 232
Minneapolis, MN 55416
877-845-8392
www.picturewindowbooks.com

Printed in the United States
of America.
Copyright © 2006 by Picture
Window Books

Special thanks to our advisers for
their expertise:

Rosemary G. Palmer, Ph.D.
Department of Literacy, College of Education
Boise State University

Susan Kesselring, M.A., Literacy Educator
Rosemount-Apple Valley-Eagan
(Minnesota) School District

Library of Congress Cataloging-in-Publication Data
Dahl, Michael.
If you were an adverb / written by Michael Dahl ;
illustrated by Sara Gray.
p. cm. — (Word fun)
Includes bibliographical references and index.
ISBN 1-4048-1357-8 (hardcover)
1. English language—Adverb—Juvenile literature.
I. Gray, Sara, ill. II. Title. III. Series.

PE1325.D34 2006
428.2—dc22
2005021857

Looking for adverbs? Watch for the big,
colorful words in the example sentences.

If you were
an adverb ...

3

Like peanut butter and jelly,
verbs and adverbs go
well together.

If you were an adverb, you would work closely with verbs.

Verbs tell us something happened. If you were an adverb, you could tell us how something happened.

The snowboarder skied GRACEFULLY down the mountainside,

but he fell **AWKWARDLY** at the bottom.

If you were an adverb, you might have a tail. Many adverbs end in the letters "ly."

How did the bear dive?

PERFECTLY

CLUMSILY

SPEEDILY

The volleyball player hit the ball SHARPLY and POWERFULLY. A player on the other side jumped FEARLESSLY into the air.

If you were an adverb, you would work at the beginning, the middle, or the end of a sentence.

RAPIDLY, the runner rounded the curve.

The runner **RAPIDLY** rounded the curve.

The runner rounded the curve **RAPIDLY.**

If you were an adverb, you could tell us how often something happens.

The long jumper **ALWAYS** jumps

The long jumper **OFTEN** jumps

more than 20 feet (6 meters).

more than 28 feet (8.5 meters).

If you were an adverb, you could tell us when something is going to happen. You could be something NOW, LATER, TODAY, TOMORROW, or YESTERDAY.

Some teams will play **NOW.**

Other teams will play **LATER.**

If you were an adverb,
you could help adjectives
describe things better.

Some athletes
are **VERY** tall.

Some athletes are
SOMEWHAT short.

Some athletes are **IMMENSELY** muscular.

Some athletes are **EXTRAORDINARILY** fast.

Some athletes are **TOO** busy practicing.

If you were an adverb, you could modify other adverbs.

The crowd watches **VERY CLOSELY** as the athletes

compete EXTREMELY WELL.

You would put together super sentences ...

... if you were an adverb!

The ADVERB GAME

Directions: Choose someone to be "it," and have that person go out of the room. Have the rest of the group choose an adverb.

Call your friend back into the room. Have your friend pick someone in the group to act out the adverb. For example, "Walk across the room like the adverb."

Your friend must watch for clues and then guess what the adverb is. Do they move swiftly or dreamily or spookily?

Your friend can pick up to three different people to act out the adverb in different ways. After three chances, explain what the adverb was, choose another person from the group to be "it," and start over.

Fact: If you look up an adverb in the dictionary, you will see the abbreviation "adv" next to it. The "adv" stands for adverb.

23

Glossary

awkwardly—doing something in a clumsy way

clumsily—doing something in a way that lacks grace

eagerly—wanting to do something very much

energetically—using lots of energy to do something

extraordinarily—doing something in a remarkable way

fearlessly—showing no fear

gracefully—doing something in a smooth manner

immensely—of great size

modify—to change in some way

Index

To Learn More

At the Library

Cleary, Brian P. Dearly, Nearly, Insincerely: What Is an Adverb? Minneapolis: Carolrhoda Books, 2003.

Heinrichs, Ann. Adverbs. Chanhassen, Minn.: Child's World, 2004.

Heller, Ruth. Up, Up, and Away: A Book About Adverbs. New York: Grosset & Dunlap, 1991.

On the Web

FactHound offers a safe, fun way to find Internet sites related to this book. All of the sites on FactHound have been researched by our staff.

1. Visit www.facthound.com
2. Type in this special code for age-appropriate sites: 1404813578
3. Click on the FETCH IT button.

Your trusty FactHound will fetch the best sites for you!

Look for all of the books in the Word Fun series:

If You Were a Noun
1-4048-1355-1

If You Were a Verb
1-4048-1354-3

If You Were an Adjective
1-4048-1356-X

If You Were an Adverb
1-4048-1357-8